1901

KRAKENOWO

OUR TOWN IN LITHUANIA

THE STORY OF A WORLD THAT HAS PASSED

Reminiscences collected to celebrate the

Diamond Jubilee of the Krakenowo

Sick Benefit and Benevolent Society

אנשי אחי עזר ד'קרקינאווע

The original cover of the book

KRAKENOWO

OUR TOWN IN LITHUANIA

THE STORY OF A WORLD THAT HAS PASSED

First Published in 1961
by the Krakenowo Sick Benefit and Benevolent Society
to celebrate their Diamond Jubilee.

Reprinted 2017

National Library of Australia Cataloguing-in-Publication entry

Title: Krakenowo the story of a world that has passed
originally compiled by the Krakenowo Sick Benefit and Benevolent Society in Johannesburg in
1961.(NB In English and Yiddish) ;
booklet now all translated into English and reprinted in English;
new booklet compiled by David Solly Sandler ;
articles translated into English by Bella Golubchik.

ISBN: 9780994619242 (paperback)

Subjects: Krakenowo Sick Benefit and Benevolent Society.
Jews--Lithuania--Krekenava--History.
Holocaust, Jewish (1939-1945)--Lithuania--Krekenava.
Jews--South Africa--History
South Africa--Emigration and immigration.

Other Creators/Contributors:
Sandler, David Solly, compiler
Golubchik, Bella, translator.
Krakenowo Sick Benefit and Benevolent Society, author.

Photo on Cover: Krakenowo as it looked before World War One

Contact for book
David Solly Sandler <sedsand@iinet.net.au>

CONTENTS

Note (1) Article was previously in Yiddish and is now translated into English by Bella Golubchik

Krakenowo - a general view of the town before World War II

FOREWORD

On the occasion of its Diamond Jubilee, the Krakenowo Society felt that it would be appropriate to have a record on paper of available information and knowledge of our forlorn old town, and if possible, one which would trace its story.

It was quite surprising how many people had photographs, information and other material referring to the community in the little Lithuanian town.

Some of these are first hand memories. Others are recollections gathered from relatives and friends. All together make a picture which is perhaps unique and is certainly valuable as a personal memento and as a historical record.

The Jewish community of Krakenowo was massacred by the Nazis. By September 1941, there were no Jews left in the town. One or two who escaped are still living in Lithuania but not in Krakenowo, one such family of survivors are settled in Rhodesia. Even the appearance of the place has changed radically.

The townspeople of Krakenowo are spread all over the world. Many of them live in South Africa, where "pioneers" and their descendants number about 400 today.

The U.S.A. has a Krakenowo society similar to ours here. There are some Jews from Krakenowo also in Argentine, Brazil, Canada, England, Israel, Rhodesia and Cuba.

Many of the Jews of Krakenowo have become distinguished in commerce, industry, mining and culture in various parts of the world.

The reminiscences in this brochure are therefore the only record, perhaps the last possible record of Jewish life in this typical East European town.

It was no easy matter to get together this material and to try and assemble a souvenir worthy of the long and commendable working not only of a society but of a community. I know you will appreciate the difficult task encountered in the compilation of the valuable material contained in this Brochure, and I therefore ask you to accept in good spirit any expressions or statements with which you may not agree, omissions, or errors in the spelling of names and places.

On behalf of the society, I should like to thank all the contributors of articles and photographs, and all those others who have helped financially to make this celebration a success.

Special thanks must go to the advertisers without whose assistance this publication would not have been possible.

My cordial gratitude goes also to Mrs. Dora Sowden for her help in proofreading the articles.

Sydney Seeff   Hon. Treasurer   1961

THE KRAKENOWO I REMEMBER *by Joseph Milne*

I was born in Krakenowo, and so was my mother, and my grandfather and his grandfather before him. Krakenowo was a village within the county of Ponevez, which in its turn was in the province of Kovno, known as Kovner Guberne. All I write about and remember occurred between the years 1900-1913, but my grandfather told me that nothing had changed for hundreds of years.

As a youngster, I regarded Krakenowo as a country on its own – to me Krakenowo was not a village at all, as we were a community who managed our affairs very well indeed. I imagined that, when the road left Krakenowo, it had reached the end of the horizon. We had no train, and, indeed, many Krakenowians had never seen a train; in fact, we did not require a train at all.

The village revolved around our revered Rabbi, who was then Rabbi Chaskin. Our Beth Hamedrash and our Shul were the largest and most beautiful buildings in the village, and we also had a smaller Shul called the Klauz. Of course we had a Chazan and two Shammosim, as well as a Kazonner Rov, which meant that he had been appointed by the Government as being responsible for the Congregation, and had to report whether the services held in the Synagogue were carried on in such a manner as not to be detrimental in any way to the policies of the Government. Our Scribe, known as Reb Hirschel, the Sefer, was well-known throughout Lithuania, and even as far afield as the large cities of Russia. I actually saw Reb Hisrchel, the Sefer, preparing the parchment for the Sifrei Torahs, and I also saw him writing the Torahs. His handwriting was very beautiful indeed, and his Torahs were famed and in great demand. There are a few Torahs inscribed by him in South Africa, and one I know of is in the Sydenham-Highlands North Synagogue, donated by Krakenowo Landsleit. Then we had a Mohel, Abraham Lazar, who had also been appointed by the Government as Registrar of Births and Deaths, to issue passports and to keep a record of men eligible for military service. In our village, there was a Schochet to slaughter our cattle and poultry in the ritual manner, but apart from these duties, he assisted in the teaching of the poorer children at the Talmud Torah.

The Russian Government maintained a Police Station in the village, with an officer in charge, whose title was "The Pristav", and any matter which required higher authority than his was referred to Ponevez, from where he received his orders. Serving under the Pristav were two ranks of Police, namely Zandar (a mounted policeman to patrol the neighbourhood) and of equal rank a Uradnik (a corporal to patrol the village on foot). Serving under these men, were several constables, called Sotniks. All the police carried revolvers, and wore curved swords. Our Jewish people feared the police very much, but also relied upon their protection at certain times, especially on marketing days. On such days many peasants came in to the village to trade, and a great deal of drunkenness ensued from their purchases of Vodka from the Government Monopol (bottle store).

Now I would like to describe how the houses were constructed in Krakenowo: they were built of timber logs, with moss laid between the logs for protection against heat and cold, and then over laid with smooth planks of wood to give a straight effect. The roofs were made of shingles. The houses had double windows, in order to give protection against the extreme cold, and the inner windows would be removed during the summer. Each window had a shutter with a bar to bolt it from the inside. Only Jews lived in the centre of the village, while the non-Jews lived on the outskirts. The non-Jews had gardens in front of their homes, but they lived in little farm-type houses, none of which could compare with the Jewish homes. Some of the poorer Jews, who could not afford to live in the centre of the village in the main streets, had very small houses with thatched roofs, in small side-streets. Because the roofs were made of shingles and of thatch there was always a danger of fire. Many villages in Lithuania were almost completely destroyed by fire, and after such disasters Balabatim would be sent from village to village to collect money to assist with the re-building of the destroyed place.

Various Societies functioned in Krakenowo to serve the interests and needs of our community. Amongst them was the "Hachnosses Kallah", to enable the poorer girls to marry, we had a "Gemillas Chesed", for the purpose of granting loans to persons in need, or requiring assistance in business. A fund existed called "Pidion Shuvuim", to provide the means of bailing out a person who had been arrested, or to assist the family of an arrested man. This fund assisted men who had attempted to avoid Russian military service, and who had been caught escaping, arrested, and forced to walk back to the village on foot as a punishment. The police would walk such men from village to village, and while they were in our village we would assist them by replacing their worn out and tattered articles of clothing, worn to shreds in the long enforced march, and by providing them with food for the journey. For the purpose of caring for and visiting of the sick, the "Bikkur Cholim" existed. These were but a few of our various Societies, established for the welfare of the community.

We had a Talmud Torah for the teaching of children whose parents could not afford to pay for their tuition. For this purpose the village had a special School-house, and employed teachers who taught the children Ivri, Chumash and Tanach. Most of the children who attended the Talmud Torah eventually learned one trade or another. Of course, we had our Chevra Kadisha, whose voluntary officials gave of their services devotedly and unsparingly. The Chevra Tillim, a Society for the reciting of Psalms, was rather an important Society, because when a baby was born, the members would visit the "kimpetoren" (the woman who had given birth), and bring her printed "Shir Hamales" (fifteen chapters of the Psalms of David). These Psalms were printed in Hebrew, and used to be hung on the walls of the room where the mother lay with the newly-born child. The members of the Chevra Tillim also used to recite Psalms when a person was seriously ill. When a death occurred, members of the Society would sit, throughout the night, reciting Psalms as well as at the funeral in our Cemetery, which was located on the other side of the River Nevyazha, running through Krakenowo. Then too, there was a "Chevra Mishneh" in the Beth Hamedrash, the members of this Society gathered around long tables each night to learn Mishneh, taught by one or other of the learned Balabatim. For those already more advanced in learning, there were the two Societies, "Ein Yakov" and "Chevra Gemorrah". And their members would also gather each night to learn a "Blat Gemorrah". It will be clearly seen from what I have written that our community was very well cared for both as regards its welfare and its spiritual life.

Krakenowo had a well-organised Community, whose motto might well have been "all for one, and one for all". As in every community, we too had our richer and our poorer people, but I do not remember, that it ever happened that a Krakenower lacked for a Challah on the Sabbath, or Matzohs on the Passover, The richer Balabatim were very charitable, and our Rabbi and the Gabboim were entrusted to assist the needy from the communal funds, without disclosing names. I recall, on many occasions, my grandmother rising very early in the morning to take some milk to people in need, or perhaps a chicken to a kimpetoren. If a Krakenower found himself in financial difficulties, our people did not hesitate: the baker, the butcher and the housewives would voluntarily bring him supplies without having to be asked. If a Krakenower lost his money, he did not have to lose his courage – assistance was soon at hand.

In the village, there was a "Kohlshe Bod" (a communal bath), and, of course, a Mikvah as well. Certain days in the week were set aside at the Bod for the use of women, but Friday was the special day set aside for men. On the allocated days our village crier called through the streets "Weiber, geit in Bod arain". On Fridays the crier had two duties to perform: at noon he would call, "Menner, gait in bod arein", and before evening he would call, "Yiddn, geit in Shul arain". As I remember, the bath was well patronised on Fridays. It was a hot steam bath, with many taps supplying hot and cold water, and shelves around the bath, upon which to sit or lie, and the higher one went, the hotter it became. When a person came to the bath, he purchased a "besem", a broom made of twigs, with which he used to beat and scrub himself, so as to remove the soil of the week. How good a Jew felt when he returned home from the Bod, cleansed and ready to go to Shul and greet the Sabbath!

Now I would like to explain how our village managed to pay for the Rov, the Chazan, the Shammas, the Schochet and for the Bod. There existed in our village a "Karobka", a monopoly over all income from kosher slaughter and over the Bod. Every two years, tenders were called for the Karobka, and the successful tenderer had to pay a certain amount of cash down as a deposit and furnish guarantees. The deposit was paid into the Treasury of the village as a guarantee that the tenderer would fulfil his contract, and the balance of the purchase prices had to be paid into the Treasury monthly, in accordance with the conditions of tender. His costs would be recouped from the sale of tickets issued by him for each and every killing, whether it be a chicken, a sheep or an ox, and the Schochet could not kill without having received the necessary ticket authorising him to do so. The ticket was valid for the date of its issue only. The Karobka money, plus the money which had been donated during the year from Aliyahs given in Shul, covered the salaries of our Communal Officials, and other communal expenditure. During the High Festivals, Aliyahs were sold to the highest bidders, and competition was keen for the honours, thus deriving considerable income. Every Jew in Krakenowo had his own seat in the Synagogue, handed down from generation to generation, so this yielded no source of revenue. There was a great deal of excitement whenever the

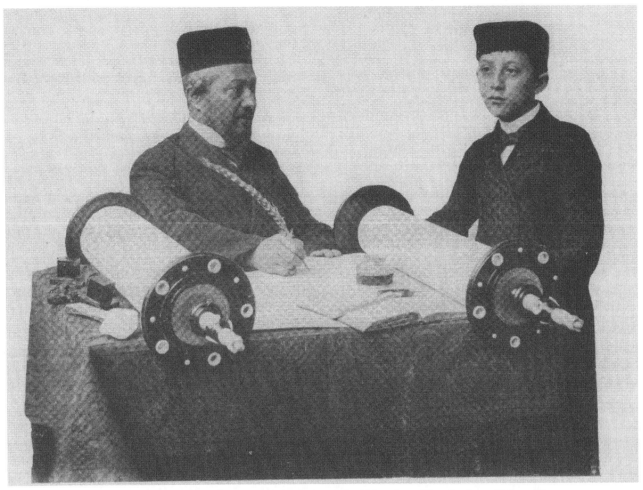

Hirshe Der Sefer - the scribe and the Sifrei Torah, with a "talmud" (pupil)

Karobka was put out to tender, and keen competition ensued. Sometimes tempers ran high and good friends became enemies, or enemies became friends, but a few weeks later, all was forgotten and forgiven, when things returned to normal. The same applied when tenders were called for the monopoly of the Bod, as there was a living to be made from being a "Bedder", the Lessee of the Bath. Such a system of communal financing may seem very outmoded now, when compared to our present-day customs in South Africa, but I feel it was most necessary and beneficial to have had the system of the Karobka in Krakenowo. It meant that the Rabbi received his salary regularly, without having to ask for contributions from the Balabatim, and he was therefore greatly respected.

The Rabbi was held in the highest esteem, and was beloved by all. He was the High Priest, and the Judge. Whenever a dispute arose, whether domestic or family affairs, or in commerce, people never resorted to litigation, but asked the Rabbi to arbitrate. If the elders of the village became aware of a dispute, the Rabbi was notified, and the parties concerned were called before him for a Din Torah, his judgement being final. Of course our Rabbi was a greatly learned and just man, while the Rebbetzin, I remember, was a grandchild of the Kovner Gaon, and admirably upheld the dignity of the Rabbi's house. On the Festivals, the Balabatim would be invited to the Rabbi's home, which was a great honour, to be entertained and to listen to his Torah and Chochme. Then the Chazan would sing melodies from the evening prayers of the Sabbath or Yom Tov, and we all joined in. Everyone felt wonderful, because he was a member of the community of Krakenowo. I recall that, on Simchas Torah, all the many Torah scrolls we had in Krakenowo were brought to the Rabbi's home. Then a procession would be formed with the Rabbi at its head, carrying a Torah, followed by the Balabatim, each carrying a Torah or a candle. The procession would wend its way through the streets, with songs of joy, to the Beth Hamedrash, where the Torah would be replaced in the Oren Kodesh. After evening prayer had been recited, the Torahs would be distributed again in the ceremony of the Hakoffesh.

But the life of the community was centred at all times round the Beth Hamedrash. Every boy could read any Maftir when he was about nine years of age. He was taught the "trop" (ritual melodies), and began to learn Chumash when he started attending Cheder. It was therefore unnecessary for a boy to receive special training for his Barmitzvah. Marriages were solemnised under the Chupah, outside the Synagogue, in the Shul Haif (ground outside the Shul). I remember that the Chosen used to wear a "kittel" (sashed white robe), and the "klezmorim" (music players) walked with all the machatonim from the Chosen's home to the Shul, and there, under the sky, the Rov and the Chazan would perform the Chupah ceremony.

Most of the wedding took place on a Friday, and after that, if the parents of the Kallah could afford it, there were seven days of rejoicing (simcha) in accordance with our law. Of course everyone in the village would send a present, mostly lekach and tort, with occasional gift of money or other valuables. Saturday night usually saw a dance in celebration of the marriage, when the musicians were paid for by the Kallah's parent up to a certain hour, but after that time the dancer paid the musicians themselves, so that they could continue dancing. There were many young people who availed themselves of the opportunity, and gladly paid for the music for dancing, as there was no occasion other than a wedding at which a Krakenower boy and girl could dance.

To our village of Krakenowo came a constant stream of Magiddim (preachers) and Meshullochim (collectors) from various Yeshivas. Sometimes there would be as many as three or four a week in our village. Those who preached in the middle of the week received a collection made for them, and for the cause they represented. Of course, an important visiting Rabbi was given the honour of making his Droshe in Shul Saturday afternoon, when the whole village would turn out to hear it.

On Sunday morning, accompanied by two Krakenowians, this Rabbi would call on the Balabatim for their yearly subscription to his Yeshiva, or for some charitable institution of Lithuania. Krakenowo Balabatim were used to these Magiddim and Meshullochim, and always donated as liberall as they could.

Then there was a continuous flow of poor people streaming daily into our village to ask for donations, and if Krakenowians had given everyone that asked a donation, they would have gone hungry themselves, so they devised a system whereby nobody was turned away empty-handed. The Balabatim used to buy metal pieces with the stamp of Krakenowo imprinted upon them and for every koppeke they received four such metal pieces. When the "ormelite" (poor people) came for donations, they would receive a metal coin, which, before leaving the village, they would cash in at the rate of four to the koppeke. Certain poor people, with large families, preferred donations of bread, and carried a bag for this purpose. Of course, Sabbath Challah was highly sought after.

Apart from the "ormelite", the Magiddim and the Meshullochim, there was another type of person who visited our village, the " Katarinshik" (Organ-Grinder), who played at every shop and house, asking for donations. All the Katarinshikkers were Jews. I do not recall a single one being a non-Jew. They travelled in pairs, a man to play the organ, and his wife or daughter to collect the money, and of course this act was never complete without a monkey or a bird.

Reverting back to the Shul - in the Beth Hamedrash , there was a "Lezankah", a long oven, very low, at the back of the Bimah, to warm up the Synagogue, and many men would gather round on winter evenings to discuss local or world politics. Legends would be told around the Lezankah, or village new repeated - this Chevra Lezankah was their radio and their television!

If a learned man, or one who had dedicated his life to the Community, died, his body would be brought into the Beth Hamedrash as a mark of honour and respect, from where it would be taken to some specially reserved place in the Cemetery. At the top of the Cemetery were the graves of Rabbonim, who had once been Rabbis of our village. Their grave were covered by a specially erected roofed structure, like a small house, as a token of the esteem and respect in which they had been held. When people were ill or in trouble, they or their families would come to pray at the house containing the graves of the Tzadikim, and ask for restoration to health, or deliverance from difficulties, begging the departed Rabbi to intercede with the Lord on their behalf.

Worshipping in the Synagogue on Rosh Hashonah or on Yom Kippur in our village, listening to the Rabbi and the Chazan, was something one could never forget - everyone turned out to attend Synagogue during the festivals and from the women's gallery one would hear wailing and sobbing. For those women who could not read the Hebrew word, there were special "zoggers", women who recited the words for them, which they would repeat, correctly on some occasions, and on others noticeably incorrectly. I remember one woman called Dobra, who intoned and recited the prayers so well, that all the other women used to gather round her and repeat her words, which she intoned with melody, and when she cried, all the women cried. This feeling and great kavonnah with which we prayed in the Krakenowo Beth Hamedrash had such an effect on my childhood and later life that, when I attended different Yeshivas in other towns and prayed in their Botei Medroshim, I felt that there was never quite the same warmth and sincerity that had existed in Krakenowo.

Whenever people of the village received bad news of Pogroms, they would gather in the Synagogue to pray with heavy hearts, and ask the Almighty to have mercy upon their fellow-Jews, and bring comfort to those who had been bereaved. The wailing and the sobbing from the women's gallery was of such sadness that it still remains distinctly in my memory. Immediately after the special prayers, a collection was made in order to send help to those of our brothers and sisters who were far away, and who had suffered at the hands of the Russian Cossacks, and by attacks of hooligans organised by the Russian Government itself. These Pogroms put fear into the hearts of our people, and caused them to seek ways and means of emigrating to America or to Africa. Some of them received assistance by way of a "billet" (ticket) to America, and some borrowed money to send their children or their

husband away, leaving the rest of the family behind, the loan being repaid as soon as money was earned in the new country and sent home. There were many good tidings at that time in Krakenowo when relative sent tickets for their families to join them, as when a Krakenower boy remembered a Krakenower girl and sent a ticket for her to come and join him as his wife. When that happened, the whole village buzzed with the good news; many girls envied her, and mothers would send photographs of their daughters to landsleit in the new country, hoping that they too would experience similar luck.

The preparations made to journey from Krakenowo to America or Africa were elaborate. A Krakenower who had perhaps never seen a train, had now to journey to a "treife" land, so far away; sending a husband or a son or a daughter to the new country was like sending them to the unknown. They felt they might never see their loved ones again. The mother of the house would bake "suchar-kes" (rusks) for the journey, as it used to take many, many days to come from Krakenowo to the nearest sea-port in Germany. There was really no scope for a young person or for a family in Krakenowo, or really any future whatsoever, and it was hard to eke out a living if one were not in business, as Krakenowo could absorb no further traders, or even artisans. The news we used to receive from those who had left our village was very encouraging. Wives would receive dollars or pounds shortly after their husbands had arrived in America or Africa, and very regularly thereafter; a mother or a wife would come to the Post Office with an American or an African Draft, feeling herself on top of the world, while less fortunate people schemed and planned to leave Krakenowo.

However, not everyone was able to leave Kra-kenowo through the usual channels, as young men over the age of sixteen were unable to obtain the necessary Exit Visas, permitting them to leave Lithuania for a foreign country, because of compulsory military service. Certain Agents were able to arrange for men to cross the border from Lithuania into Germany and many emigrants from Lithuania to America and Africa availed themselves of these channels. Those leaving Krakenowo in this manner had to journey firstly to Ponevez, where the Agent concerned was contacted and paid for his services, as well as for the ticket and all necessary documents. The Agent would then instruct the emigrant to journey to a certain border village in Lithuania, usually Yurburg, near the German border, where he would hide in a forest until the signal was given to cross the border into Germany, and the first town he came to was Tilsit. Once in Tilsit, the representative of the Agent with whom negotiations had been made furnished the ticket to Hamburg for embarkation, together with a steamship ticket to Africa, via Southhampton, or direct to America, and all other necessary documents. There was always risk, of course, attached to this means of leaving Lithuania, and if one were caught, it would have meant arrest and being marched on foot back to the village, as well as other punishment. For this reason, all tickets and documents were furnished by the Agents only when safe crossing of the border into Germany had been negotiated.

I always recall that, during the time spent in transit in Germany, we were never contacted, befriended or comforted by any Jewish Societies. German Jews dissociated themselves entirely from Lithuanian emigrants. In direct contrast, however, was the attitude of the English Jews towards us on arrival at Southhampton, and during our stay in London. We were met at the boat by representatives of London Jewry, who treated us throughout our transit period with care and consideration, which went a long way to comfort us and give us courage for the unknown that lay ahead, as we were lonely and home-sick. We were taken to a hostel in London, called the Jewish Shelter, and shown great friendship, which, I am sure, every Jewish emigrant will remember with gratitude. On arrival in Cape Town, we were again greeted by representatives of the Jewish Board of Deputies, who assisted us through the Customs and Immigration Authorities. In those days every immigrant had to be in possession of £20 in cash, so that he would not become a burden on the State. He had to be in a good state of health, with especial reference to eyes, and he had to be able to read and write one language. The Jewish Board of Deputies had intervened with the Government and had been able to arrange that Yiddish be recognised as one of the qualifying languages. This naturally assisted most of the immigrants from Lithuania, who knew no other language. From that time on, the struggle for survival in a strange, new land with a strange new language commenced. Krakenowo Landsleit emerged triumphantly, in the main, from this struggle.

There are many Krakenower in South Africa, who are Communal Leaders, and who have contributed to the mining, financial and industrial life of this country, as well as to the arts and science. Sixty years ago, when the Krakenower began to emigrate to South Africa, they founded a Krakenowo Society, and made contributions to those who had remained behind in Lithuania, as well as to newcomers to South Africa requiring assistance to enable them to make a "parnosha" (a living), so that they in turn could assist their families at home, or eventually bring them out to this country. The Krakenowo Landsleit have a most wonderful, generous and charitable background, and when one meets a Lithuanian Jew, one invariably finds him to be a warm hearted and friendly man.
It is indeed sad to think that such a wonderful community of good people, who had no quarrel with the world, who shared with their fellow-men, have lost their little village, which now exists no more. It is a tragedy that those who remained behind should have been subjected to so much pain and suffering, and their loss is a grievous one, not only to Krakenowo Jews and Lithuanian Jews, but to Jewry as a whole. No Krakenower can forget his birth place, and will always feel sad when he thinks of the fate that befell our community in our beloved little village.

We Krakenowo Landsleit in South Africa must thank God that we were spared the catastrophe which befell our little village, and that He has spared us to establish ourselves to make homes for our children in this country. We have indeed been chosen to escape the disaster, because we could no longer find any purpose in remaining in Lithuania, when there was no future for us there. I record my memories of my little village, so that the memories of our birthplace and of its inhabitants will live on for generations to come. We pass this record on to our children, and we hope that they will in turn pass it on to their children so that they too will have pride in our birth place of Krakenowo.

MEMORIES OF KRAKENOWO - AS MY MOTHER TOLD ME
by Dora Leah Sowden

There is something of a cachet about being a "Krakenower".

Perhaps the reason is that, for its size, Krakenowo has produced a more than average number of conspicuous citizens.

Perhaps it is because Krakenowo was both typical of the small town in the East European Pales of Settlement, and also exceptional in its way.

It was not an important town, yet, being a market town, it was always full of life. It was not a great business centre, yet it has produced some remarkable business brains. It was not on any arterial route, yet lying between Keidan and Ponevez, it was never isolated. It did not produce a "Gaon", yet its Rabbis and learned men were known in other centres and remembered with respect.

What makes it even more remarkable is that it was so vivid and vital as to capture the imagination of those who know it only through the minds of others.

My friend, Anita Milne, for instance, regards herself as a "Krakenower", though she was born in this country. She knows so much about "our town" from her husband, Joseph Milne, that she has adopted it.

In my case, I'm actually Krakenower born – my passport says "Craconova". Yet how much I remember of it and how much of my memories are just things my mother told me I shall never know.

My mother brought me to South Africa as an infant. It is possible (she said) that my recollections go back to babyhood. It is much more likely, however, that even the earliest "memories" are only recollections of what she said.

Our little wooden house faced the market place. I remember my mother's saying that we often got hot buns from next door. Mr. Joseph Milne has confirmed that it stood next to a bakery.

We also got new laid eggs from next door. My mother used to say that the old lady, our neighbour, used to climb up a ladder to get them from the cackling hens in the loft.

That loft (my mother said) was high, but the houses in Krakenowo were low. On one occasion, when a Russian nobleman came to our house with a lady friend, he remarked on the lowness of the roof.

Why did a Russian nobleman call at our house? Because my mother was a dressmaker- "the little woman around the corner" to the gentry who had their estates round about.

She began dressmaking at an age when her feet could not yet reach the treadle of the machine. Her sisters (she was the youngest of five) were dressmakers before her.

The aristocrats brought rich material from Petrograd and Riga and even Moscow. They sometimes brought styles from Paris and Vienna (my mother said) - special models that my mother copied.

They came in silk lined carriages, with outriders and lackeys. They often came accompanied by men friends – officers or others who showed the marks of rank.

Sometimes, they sent a troika or a britska for my mother so that she could come to their estates. In winter it was a sleigh. Sometimes she stayed a couple of days to complete a rush order.

Most of my mother's customers were Polish nobility. Only a few were really Russian. They spoke French among themselves. The women played the piano. It became my mother's idea of a refined education to be able to talk French and play the piano.

Among those of whom my mother spoke often was an old "pritsta whose little dogs always lay on pastel-coloured cushions and whined when my mother touched their mistress.

There was also a "Grafina" who was a lady-in-waiting to the Tsarina and seldom came to her estate near Krakenowo – but come she did, and then there were grand parties at the "heif".

There was the "pristav's" wife, who wanted to be a fine lady and was not above questioning my mother on what she saw in the homes of her betters.

There were the beautiful French "housekeepers" of the local priest, who complained of boredom in the country – and were replaced from time to time.

All these things were, of course, before my time, but they have become woven into the fabric of my mind.

I "remember" in this way blackbirds being shot down in the nearby woods to be baked in a pie for harvest festivals on the great estates, and cawing desperately as they fall. My mother could never after stand the sight of an injured bird in our Johannesburg gardens.

I "remember" fires across the river making the whole sky glow, and people packing their belongings in case the fire should spread, and others running about shouting "Shrekt zich nit. Gewald, es brent!" I "remember" wide green meadows, tall pine trees, turkeys to which one said "Cholder-bolder", May blossom (never identified anywhere), snow and slush and frozen lakes and deep wells.

My mother said we had a dog called "Yodka"- something frowned upon as "un-Jewish" and later given to a peasant – something for which my mother never forgave herself.

Market days (my mother said) brought the vendors of sprats, herrings, fruits and sweets.

Certainly, the delicious smell of sprats I recognised as a forgotten memory of childhood years later when I came across it in Vienna - and the herrings in Amsterdam.

Fair days reflected the mixed character of the population – the aftermath of wars and invasions.

The "Old Russians", my mother called them were few. Most of them were officials.

The Poles were the cream of the gentry. They spent their time in the big cities and came to their huge estates only in the summer. The lesser folk among them were farmers. They were the ones who came to the fairs with produce and cattle.

The Litvaks, the native peasantry, sometimes grew rich but did not count socially. The poorer ones brought fowls and turkeys to the market.

The gipsies came to sell horses, sing, dance, play and tell fortunes. Their music still has a special fascination for me. My mother always loved to have her fortune told by gipsies – and I still go to them when they are about.

Jewish traders dealt in almost everything – baigel, cloth, flounders and toys. They had inns and beerhalls. They had small shops. The local chemist was a Jew too, I think. One spoke of him with special respect.

One day the square would be empty. Then suddenly, as it seemed, there were people, booths, animals, carts – wondrous sights, wonderful sounds, delicious things to eat, to buy.

My mother used to buy whole pots of peas in the pod. Apples, sunflower and carob seeds, cucumbers and gooseberries.

Some Jews had their own smallholdings – orchards from which they brought their own fruit and vegetables. My grandfather at one time had an "allotment" of this kind (my mother said).

We Jews had a complete corporate life of our own which had nothing to do with the blackbird shooting and the harvest festivals on the surrounding estates. The market days and fairs and buying of produce from the estates and selling of large and small items to the peasants – all that was only part of this life.

There were the holy days. There was the time when one whitewashed the walls for Passover. There was the terrible moment when one opened the door for Elijah. There was the incoming of the Great White Fast.

Going to shul (said my mother) was not just routine. It was a progress. One prepared for it. Having a seder or celebrating a "simcha" was not just a party. The occasion shone with significance. The lighting of a Sabbath candle was a solemn moment. The Chanuka lamps were subjects for joy.

Thus, the tunes with which the Haggadah was intoned, the blessings made and the psalms sung have remained with me, not as conscious memories (because I was too young) but as something which when heard from a real "Krakenowo" (like Joseph Milne for instance) brings a radiance of spirit quite out of proportions to the event. Parents do not know how much they deny to their children when they deprive them of earliest impressions of sound and ceremony.

Our house had several rooms. The one in which my mother worked had a "lezanka", a brick stove like a divan, heated in the cold weather and covered with blankets. One could sit or lie on it.

Even in mid winter (said my mother) my grandmother used to get up before dawn and go and sit on the "lezanka" and read " Tilim".

My mother was never as devout as her own mother, or even her eldest sister, who wouldn't touch our doorknob with her bare hand (said my mother) because it may have been in contact with something "treif".

One story I must end with – about this same sister. My mother was still a child herself when it happened, because there were nearly 20 years between her eldest sister and herself. That sister was already married and was living with her parents – as so many young marrieds did, if the bridegroom was a "scholar".

For the young husband, the house was not "frum" enough (remember the doorknob), and there was friction.

One day, my grandmother heard of a "wonder" rabbi visiting the district. Though she did not belong to the Chassidim, she went with her daughter for advice. His immediate reply was: "Your daughter must leave the house at once". She didn't. She died within three months.

We were not above such superstitions, it seems, but of course they were only incidental to the pious and hard-working lives of our people.

Those who remember Krakenowo say that when the revolution spread and when my mother had left and the gentry in their carriages stopped coming, Krakenowo lost a lot of its romance. But that life my mother spoke of was on its way out in any case. Our departure must have been a miracle of timing – but my grandmother was left behind. She died as a war refugee in Stalingrad.

The little wooden house with the removable double windows to shut out the winter and let in the summer, already that was doomed too. My birth place was on its way into the eibigkeit.

Krakenowo as it looked before World War One

THE CLUBHOUSE *by Lazar Grazutis* (1)
(dedicated to my friends "The Resnicks)

On the right side of the street, facing the shops
Stands a wooden building, abandoned and
orphaned.
The windows and the porch weep before all,
"See here, woe is me, I am the Club"…….

The panes look out, like eyes of glass,
Bedewed, as if wet with tears,
The pale face of the shopkeeper reflected in them
As he sighs and waits for passing trade.

And there, inside, - drunkards cavort
With drunken females, in a wild dervish dance
And wild cries of joyful abandon
Are carried far and wide over the street.

And often, in the dim twilight,
When some of the shapes begin to hide away
Then slowly, dark shadows
Of evil images, begin to hover there, inside

And if you happen to glance from afar,
Then your heart trembles and beats from fear
"Where are the greatness and breadth, the pride and
the privilege"?
You ask, in pain, "Where have they gone"?

- -

But then when it's late, deep in the night
All is silent there ………. No sound is heard …….
The house is closed up, enfolded by night,
Reminiscent of bygone pride.

It seems to me that I should approach lightly,
Rap on the door : One, Two, Three,
And beloved, familiar faces
I will see once again.

And my heart draws me strongly to the porch,
I feel like leaping up ……..but, No !
The dream dissipates …….. and I hurry away,
As quickly as possible, from that Place.
Krakenowo 19 August 1912.

Notes
(1) Lazar Grazutis was one of the shtetl's intellectuals, who took an active part in all Jewish Communal life, in Lithuania in general and in Krakenowo in particular. He was renowned as a Yiddish writer and poet.
(2) Translated from Yiddish by Bella Golubchik

לייזער גראַזוטיס

דער קלוב

(געװידמעט מײנע פֿרײנד „די רעזניקס")

רעכטס אויף דער גאַס אַנטקעגן די קראָמען
שטײט עלנט פֿאַריתומט אַ הילצערנע שטוב,
פֿאַר יעדערן װײנען די פֿענצטערס, דער גאַניק:
זעט נאָר, אוי װײ איז מיר, איך בין דער קלוב…

די שױבן זײ קוקן װי גלעזערנע אויגן,
באַטויט — װי פֿון טרערן זײנען זײ נאַס,
עס טרעפֿט זײ דער בליק פֿונעם קרעמער דעם בלײכן
װאָס זיפֿצט און װאַרט אויף אַ קונה פֿון גאַס…

און דאָרט אין דעם שטוב — טאַנצן שכורים
מיט גויעס פֿאַרשכורטע אַ שדים־טאַנץ װילדן,
און קולות צוװילדערטע, פֿרײדיק־צובושעטע,
טראָגן זיך װײט איבערן געסאַלע מילדן.

און אָפֿט אין אַ גרויע טונקעלן בין־השמשות
װען עס נעמען זיך אײנצעלנע שטריכן באַהאַלטן,
דאַן שװעבן פֿאַמעלעך װי פֿינצטערע שאָטנס
אין שטוב אַרײן בײזע געשטאַלטן…

און גיט מען אויף דאָרט נאָר פֿון װײטן אַ בליק,
דאָס הארץ גיט אַ צאַפֿל, אַ טיאָקע פֿון שרעק:
די גרױסקײט, די ברײטיקייט, דער שטאָלץ און דער יחוס, —
פֿרעגט זיך מיט װײטאָק, װוּ איז עס אװעק?…

— — — — — — — — — — — — — —

נאָר דאַן װען ס'איז שפּעט, גאָר שפּעט אין דער נאַכט,
שױן שטיל דאָרט… ס'הערט זיך קיין קול…
די שטוב אַ פֿאַרמאַכטע, אין נאַכט אײנגעהילט,
דערמאַנט אָן דעם שטאָלץ פֿון אַמאָל…

און ס'דוכט זיך, מען דאַרף נאָר לײכט צוגײן
אַ קלאָפּ טאָן אין טיר : אײנס, צװײ, דרײַ
און פּנימער ליבע, באַקאַנטע,
װעל איך װידער דערזען פֿון דאָס נײַ…

און דאָס הארץ ציט אַזוי צו דעם גאַניק,
אָט װיל איך אַ שפּרונג טאָן… נאָר נײן !
דער חלום פֿאַרשװינדט… און איך אײל מיך
װאָס גיכער פֿון דאַנען צו גײן…

קראָקינאָװע, 19/8/1912.

דאָס ליד איז געדרוקט פֿון אָריגינאַל מיט אַ געענדערטער אָרט־
גראַפֿע. ר ע ד א ק צ י ע.

14

The "Kehila" of Krakenowo after World War One.
The poet of "Der Klub", Lazar Grazutis, is second from the right, standing.

Typical intellectuals of the time before World War One

KRAKENOWO 1914-1919 *by I B Stein*

August 1914 - the world seemed to change from peace and tranquillity, and our town with it. The first intimation we had of approaching war was the arrival of refugees from the border towns of Tilsit and Versbeloff. They were put up by friends.

Soon after that, all the German farmers of the neighbourhood were ordered to evacuate their farms and leave for Russia. It was said that the Government was afraid of what in later times was called a "fifth column". Their wagons were stacked high with personal belongings. The farm stock followed.

We did not realise at the time that very soon we too would have to leave our homes and most of our belonging and go deep into Russia.

The days that followed were full of excitement for the young and anxiety for the older townsfolk.

Every day there were new Government notices posted up, calling on reserves and recruits, ordering farmers in the surrounding districts to bring their horses for examination by a commissioner.

Never had our town seen so much movement of people, so many thousands of horses. Those who were passed as fit for service - men and horses - were taken to the station to be sent to Russia.

Everywhere people were discussing the war situation - even in the shul. Naturally, the main topic was who was going to win the war.

Soon, the "front" was nearing our town. The population grew more and more nervous. Shopkeepers began to pack up their goods.

One Thursday, a market day, a messenger arrived and said that the road from Sadowa to our town was full of German troops. They were advancing on our town.

Everybody started packing, putting up shutters, taking their valuables. All started moving out of the town in the direction away from the advancing Germans.

We hadn't gone far, only about a mile, when the German cavalry overtook us. We moved off the road into the ploughed fields.

Behind the cavalry came marching troops and hundreds of wagons loaded with military equipment. After that came the artillery.

The Germans did not interfere with us in any way and at nightfall we stopped at a farm off the road. All night long the troop movements continued.

At daybreak, some of us walked home to see what had happened. We found the town intact. We went back and reported what we had seen, and then everyone decided to return to the town. This was on the Friday. When we arrived back, we found that there were still a lot of German troops in the town, but they were friendly. On Saturday morning, the first shell fell in the town. The Russians had begun firing and the Germans went into retreat.

When the last of the Germans were crossing the bridge over our river, they left a demolition squad of soldiers. These put on the wooden bridge all the inflammable material they could find.

When they had rolled barrels of paraffin on to the bridge and saturated it thoroughly, they put explosives under it

By two o'clock in the afternoon of the same day, bullets began to fly overhead. The Russians were only a few miles away.

Everybody ran for shelter to the shul. It was a stone building and seemed the safest place in which to take refuge. Some people also hid in cellars belonging to one of our townsmen called Miehe Benche.

By four o'clock, the officer left in charge of the town came to tell us that the shul was not safe enough and that we must leave the town and go towards Keidan. Everybody started moving.

The older people who could not walk were put on to carts. Those who were not so religious

The Stein Family

rode on horseback. Soon the road was crowded and blocked with people.

We stopped at Yasna Gurka Mill, and when it grew dark we saw huge fires in the direction of Krakenowo. We all thought our town was on fire. People were praying. Everybody was up and awake all night.

Early next morning, several children walked back to the town to see what had happened. Then we saw that the bridge was down and smouldering, but we found that the town was

not burning and that it was empty of troops So we went back to the Mill and told everyone what we had seen. Then we all started to return home.

We had hardly reached the town when we saw Russian cavalry approaching. As they came to the bridge they asked those along the way where they could ford the river.

In the town, they demanded where the Germans were and when they had left the town. They also wanted to know where the nearest mill was and they rode straight to it. They let out the waters, and within a few hours the river was dry and the army started to cross the riverbed.

These Russians did not behave like the enemy. The first thing they did was to arrest people who had supplied the German scouts with food and drink. They arrested one woman and three men, tied them with ropes and made them run all the way to Keidan.

Next they started looting. They broke open all the shops and helped themselves to everything they wanted.

What they could not take and did not want, they invited those standing around to take away.

Market Day in Krakenowo

Fire Brigade before Word War One

One old man protested. He asked the youths not to take what did not belong to them. He was beaten up by the Cossacks and left unconscious.

Women hid in cellars and behind ovens and wherever else they could find a hiding place. It was dangerous to walk out as the Russians used whips freely and were on the lookout for anyone to beat up, for no particular reason.

It was almost impossible to hire transport to leave the town, because people were afraid to move about, but at least we managed to get out of town in a roundabout way and we went to Triscovo. A week later we heard that everyone had been ordered to leave house and home within 24 hours.

We arrived in Ponevez and found goods trains ready waiting to take us into the interior. About 30 people were crowded into each goods truck with their belongings.

We came to Swentzian, a good way from the front, and we stayed there some time. From there, my mother managed at the risk of her life to go back to Krakenowo to rescue our Sefer Torah. We took that Sefer Torah with us all over Russia and kept it in every shul we reached.

At the end of the summer, the war was approaching Swentzian too, and the Government advised all refugees to move away from the fighting line. Goods trains consisting of 15 cattle trucks were put at our disposal.

The refugees, most of whom were from our town and neighbouring places, began to organise themselves. A committee was formed. There was a doctor and nurse in charge.

As we travelled along, the committee wired to Jewish communities ahead. They gave warning that a train full of poor, hungry refugees were passing through and they asked for food.

Thus, at every station, we found on arrival Jews welcoming us with open arms and providing plenty of food.

The organisation on the journey was so good that we had a minyan twice a day.

As dozens of troop trains were going to the front, our train had often to be put on a siding. Sometimes we had to wait all day before the line was clear. At other times, the train went on without a stop for most of the day. When it did stop, we immediately got out to collect wood and make fires to cook our food. More than once the engine driver gave us a scare by starting the train without any signal, but he was only playing the fool and soon stopped again.

At last we arrived in Moscow. There we were told that the only town that could absorb refugees was Perm.

We continued on the way to Perm for weeks. We passed through many Russian towns and cities - Tula, Vologda, Viatka ...

It was in December that we arrived in Viatka. It was so freezing cold that the station master gave us a goods train with stoves and we transferred ourselves and our belongings to continue on our way.

When we arrived in Perm, we were taken to a committee centre, and there we were given a wonderful welcome as we were the first refugees to arrive there. But as the housing problem was acute, we were advised to go by boat to the town of Solikamsk.

Never had we dreamt that so far away from home, deep in the Ural mountains we would find such warm-hearted people as those who welcomed us in Solikamsk. When the boat brought us to the nearest landing, we saw dozens of sledges coming towards us. They put our luggage on the sledges and brought us to the town. The streets were lined with people. There were placards and banners across the streets saying "Help the poor and hungry refugees."

We were taken to a school building. Tables were laid with plenty of food and drink. They overwhelmed us with their kindness.

Afterwards, we were taken to barracks where each family was allowed one room, and each member of a family was given a weekly allowance and food.

Later we asked them to find us other living quarters. This they did rent free. They even supplied us with wood as it was mid-winter and bitterly cold.

Tradesmen received tools, tailors were supplied with machines, and butchers were given shops. We settled down in earnest to a peaceful existence.

We were sent to Russian schools and even had a Hebrew teacher - a Jew, of course.

The first thing the committee did was to find a suitable place for a shul. In one of the adjoining huts, a mikvah was built.

Every Saturday was market day. Then the farmers from the surrounding districts brought in frozen fish and vegetables - and fox skins. With the permission of the spiritual leader, the Jewish shopkeepers and tradesmen were allowed to take part on the market day.

We stayed in Solikamsk for eighteen months and then moved to Tsaritzyn (now Stalingrad) where we remained for two years. From there, we went back to Krakenowo in 1918.

We found the town burnt to the ground, the whole place overgrown with tall weeds. Only the cellars were visible.

The Germans had removed the stones from the foundation of the house to repair the roads.

It was difficult to recognise the place where our house had stood.

Many of the shopkeepers built wooden huts on their stands. In the morning the goods were brought in baskets and at night were taken back to the dwelling places, as the huts were not secure enough for goods to be left in them. In winter, some practical jokers even used to move the huts and put them in the cellars. After a night of heavy snow, they were hardly visible.

Soon more people arrived from Russia. Gradually the town was built up. No one, of course, thought of a luxury home – just four walls and a roof. Several people shared homes.

Yet all those who returned were happy to be back after so much wandering in Russia.

Bridge across the Neviaze

KRAKENOWO SICK BENEFIT AND BENEVOLENT SOCIETY

DIAMOND JUBILEE CELEBRATION

NORTH EASTERN COMMUNAL HALL

1st NOVEMBER, 1961.

PROGRAMME

TOAST	The Republic of South Africa. The State of Israel.
WELCOME	Dr. Harvey Cohen.
MESSAGES	S.A. Jewish Board of Deputies Mr A J Rajak S A. Zionist Federation Mr J Rubik
SOLO DANCE	Miss Jose Ora Druker
GREETINGS	Mrs A Galgut
SONG RECITAL	Mr Ben Stein *Kindly accompanied by Mr Marcus Levy*
TOAST	The Krakenowo Society: Mr B. Gering Reply: Mr J Goldman

TEA

MUSICAL INTERLUDE BY BENNY MICHEL AND HIS BAND.

VIOLIN SOLO	Mr. Gus Levy *Kindly accompanied by Mr Marcus Levy*

GUEST SPEAKER OF THE EVENING: MRS ANITA MILNE.

SONG RECITAL	Cantor Philip Badash. *Kindly accompanied by Mr Marcus Levy*
PRESENTATIONS	Mr Barney Levin Mrs Hilda Lax
VOTE OF THANKS:	Mr Woolf Cohen

TISH'A B'AV 1914 - 9th OF AV – 1914

A letter from Mr Joe Resnick, son of the renowned Micha Resnick of Krakenowo. He travelled from Johannesburg for a visit to his home shtetl, on the eve of the First World War and couldn't return to South Africa due to the outbreak of the War.

Dear Dina

I have received your letter and thank you for your prompt reply to mine.

Today is Tish'a BeAv. Jews are fasting. Jews worldwide are mourning the destruction which took place thousands of years ago, but the destruction here is much worse. Mothers mourn their sons, children mourn their father, all of whom were taken away by the mobilization.

There is a great upheaval caused by the imminent European War. We were informed on Monday about the ultimatum which Austria presented to Serbia. The situation worsened on Tuesday and Wednesday. Anyhow, you are probably better informed about this in Johannesburg, as you don't have censorship.

While strolling down Keidaner Gass on Tuesday evening we noticed the Priestov, the officer in charge of the police station, and the parish scribe running frantically around, and subsequently they entered the Post Office, where they remained for about half an hour, then they rushed out, one, into the administration office and the other into the Parish office. It wasn't even fifteen minutes later, when riders on horseback were racing to the villages. No one knew what this was all about, but we assumed they were rushing to announce the mobilization. Just imagine! I woke on Friday morning early and saw clusters of people on the street. I dressed hastily and ran down and saw placards displayed, announcing the mobilization of servicemen; also "Red Tickets" which were never before issued concurrently with the first mobilization, only after the second mobilization. By ten o'clock in the morning, numerous Christians had gathered, together with their horses and wagons. This was because horses and wagons had also been mobilized. They finished at ten o'clock at night.

It was like the biggest fair. They stood, one on top of another, from Yankel Boruch as far as the Priest, over the whole length of Keidaner Gass. They instructed all the appropriated horses and carts to wait until Shabbat morning and they were then sent away to Poneveszh with supplies. It was a heartbreaking scene watching them ride away on Shabbat morning.

Mothers and children shed rivers of tears. The noise of weeping was deafening. One of the gentile women fainted, when they took her three sons away. She had no other children.

There were nineteen Jews, among whom was Yoseh, Ortzik's; Shayah, Abba's, and Hirsheh, the blacksmith. There was some hope, that they might possibly be released, as they were all older than 42 years. Also, Avrom Yitzchak Chaim Hirsheh, the butcher's son. I don't know any others. The remainder were in the school yard. Itzik, Bereh Mingelaner's son-in-law was among the reserve.

The banks stopped paying out on Friday. Until Friday they were still paying a percentage. Currently they are not meeting any promissory notes. There is a tremendous uproar. The Kovner Gubernyeh is in wartime mode. Last Tuesday they gave the inhabitants of Kovno three days to vacate. They locked their businesses and fled. There are no passenger trains. They are all packed with military. Meanwhile, they have transferred the government to Poneveszh. Even the governor is there. They have also transferred the Treasury to Poneveszh, and relocated the Warsaw Treasury to Lebo.

Some of the Jews tried to steal across the border from Poneveszh, but a number of them were shot.

Getzel Galaskis' children have just arrived from Kovno. They say that they stayed on the station from Thursday till today and only managed to get a ticket on a freight train today. In the interim they have mobilized fighters in 42 areas, but they say that if a Peace deal is not concluded there will be a second conscription. Then it is possible that I too ………

I wish that I could write you some news but who can contemplate that today.

My money is in Poneveszh. If there is a peace deal, they may still pay it out, and if not, one can say "Goodbye"……

Joe Resnick

Krakenowo 20 July 1914

Notes
(1) : This letter was reprinted from the original
(2) Translated from Yiddish by Bella Golubchik

I MARRIED A KRAKENOWER *by Anita Milne*

I married a Krakenower, and I am very proud of it. Although I was born in Johannesburg, my husband's background of life in his village, Krakenowo, and the tradition of Lithuanian Jewry, has had a great influence on my life and on my home. I can as clearly visualise the life of Krakenowo, and the life in the Lithuanian villages, as if I had lived there myself. This is because my husband has told and retold me so often of the interesting Jewish life lived in Lithuania, and has told me so much about his village. I have a great respect for the background of Lithuanian Jewry. Time and again, when I speak of Krakenowo, people ask me whether I have ever been there that I know so much about it and its customs. When I was a little girl, I remember my mother telling me that if I were able to marry a Lithuanian Jew, I would be well cared for by a man who would always earn a living, and respect and love his family. I am glad I heeded her advice: time has proved her to be so right.

My husband is a very religious man: he is the son of a Rabbi, who was in his turn the son of a Rabbi. When I married my husband he made me the custodian of something which he treasures greatly, and that is his father's Smicha (Rabbinic certification) – a Smicha from four great Rabbis, amongst them being the Smicha from Reb Yitchok Elchonon, known as the Kovner Gaon, who was the greatest Jewish sage, I understand, of the last century. My husband has told me how he came to be in possession of this Smicha. When his parents were forced to flee from Lithuania, all they saved from their great wealth was the Smicha and their Sifre Torah, which to them were their most valuable possessions. His father died on the journey, but his mother managed to reach the Ukraine. The Communist Government made things extremely difficult for Rabbis and for religious people, so his mother thought it would be safer to send the treasured Smicha to her son in South Africa, who she knew would value it greatly, and so it was sent to him for safe keeping. Of course, the Torah could not be sent as well, so it had to be hidden.

My husband was a Yeshiva Bocher, and his father had great hopes that he would carry on the unbroken family tradition, and become a Rabbi too one day. At the age of eight years, he was already attending Yeshiva, amongst bochurim far more senior in years than he – some even double his age. His parents and teachers hoped that he would one day become a great Rabbi in Jewry. He has told me that to have attended the Yeshiva in those days was a vastly different matter than to study in a modern

Yeshiva today. The custom then was to board out the Yeshiva Bochurim – this system was called "essen teg" – and the Balabatim of the town where the Yeshiva was situated would gladly provide meals for the bochurim on the various days of the week. If a Yeshiva Bocher was able to have a tog with various Balabatim on each of the seven days in the week, he could count himself fortunate indeed: However, the bochurim had provision made for them on about four to five days in the week in most instances, and the other few days they would be hungry. The Balabatim fed the bochurim as their own families, but some had very little even for themselves, yet they gladly provided a meal for one who studied Torah. I can never forget one instance which my husband told me happened to him. Butter was provided for his at a meal he was having at the home of one of his Balabatim, but no bread upon which to spread it, and he was too shy to ask. He waited and waited, but as no bread was forthcoming he did not wish to go away hungry and leave the butter unused as well, so nothing daunted young Joseph proceeded to smear the butter on has hard, sturdy boots to soften them!! Instead of food, some of the Balabatim preferred to give the bochurim money – ten to fifteen koppekes – for the tog. While studying at the Vilna Yeshiva, my husband was provided with two teg during the week, for which he was given the money instead of food: one day was given by Rabbi Akiva, a Dayan of Vilna, and the other by a Wholesale Hardware Merchant, both uncles of the late Chaim Gershater, former Editor of the Zionist Record, who was himself a Krakenowo.

Shortly before Mr Gershater's death, my husband asked him what had happened to his uncles, and was told that the one who had been a Vilner Dayan had died, and the other uncle, who had been a merchant, had fled to Siberia during the war, and had only fairly recently been repatriated to Poland, and from there to Israel. My husband then said, "You know, Mr Gershater, I owe your uncle money, because he provided me with the means to essen teg for two years in Vilna, and I would like to repay him". Mr Gershater was very touched, and the very next day he received a cheque for his uncle in Israel, which gave my husband a great deal of pleasure and gratification to be able to repay an old debt.

Then, too, the bochurim would sleep on the hard benches at night in the Yeshiva, providing their own mattresses made of straw, and each had a cushion brought from home. No dormitories for them, as in modern Yeshivas! There were no hours for studying – they started early in the morning, as soon as the sun was up, and continued until late at night. Some of the Yeshivas had hostels for the students, as in Vilna and in the Ramales Yeshiva, where accommodation was provided for the bochurim, but the system of "essen teg" was the same everywhere. The students studying in these Yeshivas gained a great deal of knowledge and learning, which stood them in good stead all through their lives. Whenever I come into my husband's library, where is housed his great collection of Talmudical Books and Hebraica, and see him studying, as he often does, with his yarmelke upon his head and completely absorbed by what he is reading. I realise that he is still the Yeshiva Bocher at heart!

Through him, I became very interested myself in the life of the Lithuanian Jewry, and learned all I could on the subject.

An unusual story of Krakenowo of which my husband has told me involves his own family, and bears, I think, retelling. It is the story of his grandmother, whose son one day mysteriously disappeared from Krakenowo and was not heard of again for eight years. Of course after his disappearance, Kaddish was recited for him, and it was truly felt that he would never be seen again. But eight years later, he wrote to his mother, telling her that he had done very well for himself, and was domiciled in Waco, Texas, in the United States of America. He begged his mother and father to come there and live with him, or if not, at least to visit him. One can well imagine the great Simcha when these glad tidings came, but the grandmother, being a very religious woman indeed, hesitated to travel to this foreign land. After much discussion, it was decided that her husband should go to Texas first to visit his son, and then return to Krakenowo. In those days, the undertaking of such a journey was a tremendous adventure, and the grandmother feared that her husband might not return, through suffering some hazard on the journey, and not be heard of for many years, if at all, as had happened to her son. It was therefore decided to go to the Rabbi and obtain a "Tnai Get" (conditional divorce) – if her husband were to return within a certain time, the "Tnai Get" would be declared null and void, but should he fail to return within the specified time, the "get" would be enforced, and they would be legally divorced. His grandmother was then still a young woman, and did not wish to remain an "Agunah" (a woman whose husband has left her, but is not able to obtain a get), and thus be precluded from marrying again. Well, the husband, in fact, did not return to her within the specified time, and the "get" came into force. She married again, and my husband's mother was the

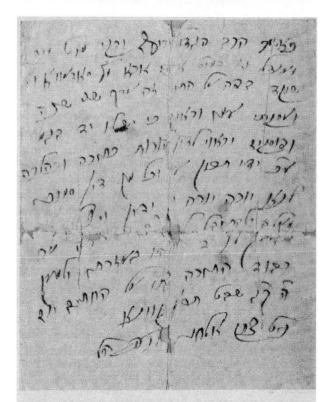

כאשר הרב הגדול חריף ובקי מו"ה מנחם מענדל נ"י במו"ה אברהם אבא מק' סאדאווא שוקד בפה על התורה זה ערך של שנה ועסקתי עמו וראיתי כי יש לו י"ד בגמרא ופוסקים וראוי לדון ולהורות כתורה וכהלכה על כן ידי תכון עמו וכל מן דין סמוכו לנא יורה יורה ידין ידין ויעלה מעלה מעלה ——— וד' יהי' בעזרתו ולמען כבוד התורה באתי על החתום יום ה' כ"ב שבט תר"ן קאוונא. נאום יצחק אלחנן החופ"ק הנ"ל.

Facsimile of the Rabbinical Certificate (Smicha) awarded to Mr. Joseph Milne's father by the world renowned Gaon Rabbi Yitzchak Elchonon from Kovno, and on the following page is another Smicha by Rabbi Yitzchak Meier from Slobodka.

Partial translation of the Smicha above by Bella Golubchik

The great rabbi, wise and erudite, our teacher and rabbi, Menachem Mendel, may his light shine brightly, (son) of our teacher and rabbi Avrohom Abba, of the congregation of Sadowa, industrious in Torah. I have studied with him and engaged with him, and ascertained that he has authority in the Gemorrah and the commentators, and is worthy to legislate and teach Torah and Halacha.

Thus he is empowered by this S'micha to educate and to judge, and to succeed and may HaShem aid him for the sake of the honour of the Torah.

I hereby sign this on Thursday 22nd Shevat TaRan (5650) 1890 – Kovno
Yitzchak Elchanan

only child of this marriage. Of course his father got "nadan" (dowry) and many years "kest" (board and lodging) from her parents, as was the custom when the son in law had his Smicha, so that he could continue his studies uninterruptedly. Many years later, the grandmother did journey to Texas upon her son's continued insistence that she visits him, and he even sent a man especially from America to escort her. Upon her arrival at her son's home, she met her previous husband, who had made his home there, and she immediately left her son's home, refusing to spend even one night under the same roof as her ex husband, and lived in another house during her stay in Texas. After a while, she left America, as she felt it was not a sufficiently religious way of life for her, and she returned home to Krakenowo and to her only daughter, my husband's mother. But her son gave her many presents before her departure, and she returned home with golden chains, jewellery and many valuable articles. A firm arrangement had been made with her son that he would send her money twice a year, on Rosh Hashonah and on Passover, and as long as his mother was alive he honoured his promise and undertaking. Originally, my husband had intended to go to this uncle in Texas to settle, but a change in plans brought him to Africa instead, as he had an aunt living here.

My husband is a very keen gardener, and he tells me that in Krakenowo his home in Keidaner Gass had a very large garden, and his grandmother gave him a small piece of this garden for his very own, provided he looked after it. This he did very well indeed, and it was the beginning of his love for gardening which has persisted to this day. His grandfather had a small holding on the outskirts of Krakenowo, where wheat was grown, and immediately this was reaped, portion of it was stored in a barn, until it was made into special flour for Passover. The matzos made from this particular wheat were called "shmurroh", which meant that it had been watched from the moment it was harvested until it was taken to the miller. Rabbi Chaskin, the Rabbi of Krakenowo, and my husband's father, were present during the baking of these matzos. The Balabatim would then come and each take six matzos from the Rabbi, knowing that this was the special "shmurroh matzoh", and it was always used for the three traditional matzos over which the Brocha is recited on each of the two nights of Passover, and from which the afikomen was taken.

When Passover is celebrated each year in our home, and we are surrounded by relations and friends, my husband intones the words and melodies of the Haggadah with traditional Krakenowo "niggun" (melody), and his beautiful voice rendering the nostalgic melodies our people have known and loved for so many generations is deeply moving.

Although Krakenowo is now no more, its spirit still lives and breathes wherever its landsleit find themselves. The very fact that my husband, Krakenowo born, has been able to convey so much of its spirit, its tradition and its background to me, South African born, that I feel myself a Krakenower by adoption, is ample evidence that Krakenowo still lives in the minds and hearts of those who hail from there.

Partial translation of the Smicha above by Bella Golubchik

The great rabbi, wise and erudite.....our teacher and rabbi, Menachem Mendel, from the holy congregation of Sadowa, has diligently studied at the portals of Torah, has devoted much time to Gemorrah and Tosafot (annotations to the Talmud)............... he has great knowledge in law and teaching. I intend to make this known by all, that he is worthy to be an educator and legislator in Israel and to give him S'micha to teach and judge among the most distinguished of Rabbonim.

The place which gives him the position of Rabbi, will reap Naches from him as he is very G-d fearing, and it is commendable to try to help him, as he will succeed and go from strength to strength.

Wednesday 10th Adar Sheini TarMat (5649) 1889

Signed: Rabbi Yitzchak Meier   Slabodka

MY SHTETL KRAKENOWO by Y. GELL

No other shtetl in all Lithuania had what Krakenowo had, a river flowing through it. The Neviaze divided it in two: green fields and forests. On one side, the Delugas; on the other, the Taletnik, the local forest, the Freiver forest and the Ramegoler forest. In these woods there grew wild strawberries, raspberries, blackberries, blueberries, various other berries and nuts and also Turkish nuts. One could pick as much as one's heart desired.

In the summertime, the whole shtetl bathed in the Neviaze. They bathed the horses and submerged the wagons during the Shabbat to soak a little, to prevent their creaking or disintegrating. In the winter, the youth skated on the ice. They also used to launder the washing on the ice . There was always some activity involving the river.

Krakenowo had 300 Jewish families, all dear, honest observant Jews. We remember them with affection. It also had a beautiful Beit Medrash, a Shul, a small shul and shtieb'lach, a Yeshivah with fifty bocherim, a Rabbi, a Chazan, a Shocheit, a doctor and a felsher, two Pharmacies and a Public Bath, a hospital for the poor and a Fire Brigade.

Also, there were Societies: Lomdei Torah Society, Ein Ya'akov Society, Menorat HaMa'or Society, The Chevra Kadisha, Linat Tzedek Society, Tif'eret Bachurim Society, The Chevra Mishna Society, Chevrat T'hilim Society, G'miluth Chesed, The Hachnasat Kalah Society and others. Each society had Chairmen and committee members. They were all occupied with shtetl communal work, all week.

Everyone there, had a name and a nickname:

Yankel, the Pope;	יאנקל דער פּאָפּס
Yoshe, the Nose;	יאָשע דער נאָז
Shaya, the Cat;	שייע די קאַץ
Ortzik, the Kaizer;	אָרציק דער קייזער
Itzeh, the Soldier; and	איטשע דער סאָלדאַט
Gruneh, the Itch.	און גרונע קראַץ.

Berkeh, the Constable; Yisroel-Sh'mulkeh, the Candlestick; Avremkeh, the Mamzer (Bastard); and Elkeh, the Peasant.	בערקע דער סאָטאַניק ישראל־שמולקע דער לייכטער און אבעלע באו אוורעמקע דער ממזר עלקע דער פּויער און שמולקע די שאו.
Leibeh, the Pampered; Dovid, the Pipe; Gershon, the Bovine tail; Shifrah,	לייבע די פּילוע דוד די פּיפּקע און גרשון דער ציגענער עק. שיפרה די פּאַווע שלמה די אלמנה און אָרציק דער גרעק.

the Peahen; Shalmah, the Widow; and Ortzik, the Chignon;

Leizer, the Bread giver; Lipkeh, the Comet;

Pesach, the Fireman; Tzalkeh, the Stingy; Idel, the Wise; Moteh Sholem, the Kozak; and Mosheh Sholem the Stepladder.

לייזער דער ברויט־געבער ליפּקע דער קאָמעט און פּסח דער פּאָזשאַרניק. קנאלע דער פּאָפּוז דוד דער פּאָסטוך און מייער דער אָראָדניק.
צאָלקע דער פּאַרך אידל דער חכם און מאָטע־שלמה דער קאָזאַק. אברהם דער קאָנפּעטירניק משה־שלום דער לייטער און איצקע דער בורלאָק.

And so forth.

However, the Society which caused the most trouble in the shtetl, was. The Ganovim Society- The Thieves' Society. The biggest thief was Reizeh Yankel's goat. Not only was she a thief, she was also a robber too. No sooner than the goat had opened her eyes, she began lifting whatever she could. There was a certain Jewish woman, who stood in the marketplace, selling beigels. The goat sneaked up and snatched a beigel. When somebody tried to take the beigel from her, or to chase her away, she raised herself up on her hind legs and prepared to fight to the death.

There was nothing that could be done about Reizeh Yankel's goat, because it constituted her only income. The goat supplied the whole shtetl. Reizeh Yankel's had the milk and cream, and also sufficient left over to sell. However, HaShem, Blessed be His Name, doesn't abandon a whole Jewish Shtetl.

One summer's evening, shouting was heard : Reizeh Yankel's was alight . Fire! Help! Jews, Save me!

The Fire Brigade , with its new "machine" and with two tanks of water and long hoses, helmets and broad belts with hatchets, came rushing to Reizeh Yankel's house. "Fire! Jews, Save me!"

When they entered the house, they saw the goat stretched out on the ground and Reizeh, lying on top of her, pleading : "Jews, help! A fire broke out, and my breadwinner is expiring".

It didn't take long and the goat breathed her last. The Fire Brigade loaded the goat on to the new *machine* and accompanied her on her way. And thus, my shtetl Krakenowo got rid of the town *ganef* – Reizeh Yankel's goat

Itzeh Moshe Avrom Leizer's or Itzeh the Burlak. (The Bargeman)

Translated from Yiddish by Bella Golubchik

*The **Neviaze** River and the town forest*

A football team in Krakenowo

26

A FEW WORDS ABOUT MY SHTETL *by A Shaban*

Moshe Nadir once said : "My Shtetl, how deeply I love you and how strongly I hate you". A comment worthy of note. I have the same feelings for my shtetl, Krakenowo. I love it and hate it at the same time.

It is close on 35 years that I left it , but still today, when I shut my eyes, I see the whole shtetl before me, as if it were but yesterday.

In front of me I see the main road, Keidaner Gass, a long street, that divides the shtetl in two equal parts, one on either side of it, through the whole length of the town. There are houses and wooden shacks, with straw or shingled roofs, and with only one exception, Micha's building, an edifice, actually built of mortar and brick. And here, the road bisects the Poneveszher Gass like a Crucifix, from Mottel Malkah's house, across the bridge and over the hill, to the house of Moshe, the teacher. There, around

on earth.

Then, suddenly, I see Winter in the shtetl. The roads and lanes are covered in snow. The thatched roofs are white, as if painted in thick white paint. The window panes depict frosty pictures. Crows tap dance on the branches of the trees and croak with bloodcurdling noises. Their croaking blends with the lonely twilight tolling of the church bells and the sound of the squeaking of the boots of Jews on their way to Mincha.

Now, before my eyes, I see my shtetl, in its summer glory and its white wintery cold, in its spring playfulness and deep autumnal mire and oh, so much mud.

Perhaps Krakenowo was not more beautiful, not better, not cleaner nor dirtier, than any of the other shtetlach in Lithuania.

Before the First World War, Krakenowo had Chedorim, a Yeshivah, illustrious Rabbis and Rosh Yeshivas and decent, respectable Yeshivah students, and a few enlightened folk who tended towards the outside world.

After the First World War, and before the outbreak of the Second World War, Krakenowo had a modern Hebrew School, beautiful, enlightened youth, a Sports Club, a decent library, drama groups, a Civic Council, a Peoples' Bank and so forth.

Yes, Krakenowo also had an import export business. They exported geese to Germany and children to Africa, Israel and America. The imports consisted of pounds from Africa and dollars from America.

Life in my shtetl Krakenowo reminds me of one long yawn. Everything moved along slowly, languidly, as if nothing moved out of alignment and even the wind behaved moderately. It would enter the holes in torn trousers slowly and then at a still slower pace, leave through the holes in torn shoes. It used to enter the chimney stack on the roof slowly and sniff the Lokshen-Kugel and the Shabbat Cholent, and then slowly push its way through the closed mouth of the oven, kiss the modest faces of the Jewish daughters, caress their freshly washed hair and long plaits and then silently disappear.

And so, my shtetl lived in an idyllic manner, until there came The Great Holocaust, the Hitler catastrophe. The Bestial Nazis together with the Lithuanian Hooligans, came and destroyed my shtetl and obliterated the Jews.

My shtetl is no more.

My Jews are no more.

Translated from Yiddish by Bella Golubchik

1920 TO 1930 – THE BEGINNING OF THE END *by Percy Zelikow*

The period between 1920 and 1930 was of both significance and importance in the life of the Jews of Krakenowo. The newly established Republic of Lithuania, after decades of oppression under the Czarist regime, surged forward, spurred by a fervent nationalism and cultural awakening. In all spheres of its national life – in politics, culture, sport, as well as in the economic field – the new Lithuania strove to make up for lost time and to catch up with the more developed West.

This also had its effect on the Jews of Lithuania, who, like their neighbours, were fired with the desire to develop their own national character. In Krakenowo we see tremendous activity during the decade. The newly formed Beth Sefer Ivri, based on the Tarbuth educational system, attempted to give the children a modern education in the Hebrew medium. A library was soon established which was well stocked with modern books, and the youth were able to acquaint themselves with the Russian, German, French and English classics, as well, of course, as with the best Yiddish and Hebrew literature. The library was not only a place where books were lent: it also served as a club where the youth would meet to discuss the books they were reading, and as a hub of social life.

From the library sprang a cultural society which offered lectures on a variety of subjects. The lecturers were mostly local talent – the school teachers, some of the better informed local youth – but once in a while a stranger from Kovno or Ponevez would put in an appearance and give additional stimulus to the discussions of a favourite topic. Little Krakenowo had a big cultural appetite. Books were simply devoured by the readers. The subject matter of the lectures was rather lofty. In fact, a Kovno lecturer once remarked that the discussions were somewhat esoteric – but Krakenowo did not care. Ordinary day to day matters interested them less than subjects such as Dialectical Materialism and its interpretations of history; Hellenism and Judaism; Zen-Buddhism and Christianity. Bible criticism was a popular subject, and of course, the constant, never ending discussion of nationalism, religion and sex.

The management of the Jewish Community – comprising at its height some 300 families – was in the hands of the Kehilla. This was a democratic body elected by all the residents. There were no property or educational qualifications and every Jew in Krakenowo had the right to vote. The annual meetings were stormy and elections were most exciting, but candidates were judged purely on their personal merits. There were no parties.

The Kehilla committee, once elected, would meet weekly and the locale was a room in our house. So I would have an opportunity of listening to the deliberation and discussions. The "tongeber" was Moshe Aaron Rabinowich, a miller who lived just outside the shtetel. He was the brain and the leading intellect, and during the voting in committee one would frequently hear; "I vote the same as Moshe Aaron". Particularly conspicuous was a certain balabos who did not have the ability to concentrate and in most cases did not know what the discussion was all about. Nor was there any need for him to break his head about it. Whatever opinions "Reb Moshe Aaron" happened to hold was good enough for him.

One of the tasks of the Kehilla was the mobilisation of foreign aid – that is, to turn to the Krakenowo Landsmanschaften in New York and in Johannesburg for financial aid to build a "Bod" (public bathing place); to reconstruct the burnt down Beth Hamedrash; to supplement the Rabbis salary which the community could not carry itself. I recall as a little boy slanting over the shoulder of a young man who, seated at a table in our house, was writing a long and flowery letter in a beautiful calligraphic handwriting to America for funds for some cause. The young man who made such a great impression on me, both with his intelligence and with his handwriting, was the late Chaim Gershater. As it turned out, writing was destined to be his life's career.

An interesting personality in the life of the Kehilla was Lazar Grazutis, who later married my sister Chana, and subsequently perished in the Kovno Ghetto. Grazutis was the secretary of the Kehilla. He was also the secretary of the Volksbank, the local

A group of friends - Top: P Zelikow, I Kier, Zlotiapko, Laz Tocker and Sydney Seeff.
Bottom: Unknown, A Mervis, Ch Friedman and S Pogir

Jewish credit bank, and in addition to this he served for a time as director of the school. Among these three institutions there was a regular exchange of correspondence, dealing with their various negotiations and transactions. As general secretary of all three institutions, Grazutis would often have the peculiar task of writing letters from himself to himself. Being a man with a brilliant sense of humour, he would sometimes for sheer devilment incite some committee member against the secretary of one of the other institutions to which he gave his divided services. In his wrath, the committee member would be heard to say, in rather strong language: "write him a letter and tell him, the so and so".

The youth of Krakenowo fell into two main groups: the Zionists and the anti Zionists. These two groups differed not only in their ideology, but also represented two different social strata. The richer, the "balibatishe jugend", the sons of merchants – they were the Zionists. The others – the tradesmen, the workers, the "baalmeloches", with a sprinkling of the intelligentsia amongst them – were the anti Zionists. The Zionists were organised in the local Maccabi; the others were known as Yak (Yiddishe Atletik Klub). Both derived added inspiration through propagandists from the larger centres, who made an appearance from time to time and confirmed their belief in the righteousness of their respective ideologies.

In the field of sport, however, there was no separation. Both sections of the youth swam together in the Neviazhe, took long walks in the forest and played football in organised teams. Soccer was, of course, the popular sport and became most competitive when played against the teams of neighbouring villages. There is a story, for the veracity of which I cannot vouch, which refers to a match that once took place between Krakenowo and Ramigole. The game was keen and fierce, with the inevitable fist fight towards the end. Whilst the attack was first directed against the referee, it later developed into a free for all, involving both players and spectators. Let it be said to the credit of both Krakenowo and Ramigole that order was eventually restored, tempers cooled off, and a very amicable settlement was arrived at – a settlement which satisfied both sides, though it was rather unorthodox and probably unequalled in the history of soccer. It was agreed that the goal in dispute be shared equally by the opposing teams, and both Krakenowo and Ramigole happily rejoiced with a final score of 2 ½ – 2 ½.

Notwithstanding the apparent full-bloodedness of the life of the youth, there was, however, a constant, ever present feeling of hopelessness and frustration. The younger generation had no vision of any economic future for itself. The life of the Jewish

The wedding of Rivel Seeff to Rabbi Woolf Kuznec in Krakenowo in 1934, with the parents of the bride, Mr and Mrs Woolf Seeff, at the main table.

A group of Krakenowo Youth

shopkeeper was so unattractive to his son that he had no intention of following his father's means of parnosse. The tradesman, the "baalmelocha", hardly eked out a living; his son surely was not tempted to make his father's trade his career. Those who left Krakenowo to study at Kovno University never came back to the shtetel.

In addition to the hopelessness of the economic position, there was the everlasting problem of anti-Semitism, which flared up anew with the rise of the Lithuanian youth movements, which was nationalistic and chauvinistic in character. There was clearly no prospect for the Jewish youth in the villages and small towns of Lithuania, nor in the cities for that matter. The answer was – emigration. A strong movement of chalutziut developed. Young boys and

Mordechai Varkel (standing right), a teacher and PT instructor, at an athletic performance of the Krakenowo Hebrew School.

girls spoke Hebrew, and sang the New Hebrew songs which gave them hope and inspiration. Their goal was Palestine. It was they who formed the backbone of the Chalutz Movement, who established settlements and kibbutzim in Palestine, who dried the swamps and developed the land. Krakenowo contributed its share of chalutzim. A number of young men and women also immigrated to other faraway lands in search of pastures new, wider horizons and fresh hope. The "potchtalion" (postman) now began to bring letters and "passilkes" from Canada, from Cuba and most of all from South Africa. Those who had remained behind were infected with a restlessness, a dissatisfaction, and were eager to pull up their roots from the shtetel which, though full of sweet memories, held nothing but frustration for the future. Then came the news that in South Africa anti immigration laws was being promulgated which would come into force at the end of 1929. That gave additional impetus to the stream of emigration, and the third class of the Union Castle Liners leaving Southhampton for South Africa were now filled to capacity with young men and women from Lithuania. The shtetel was emptied of its youth. The romantic songs that used to echo through the village every Friday night were heard no more. The fortunate ones had gone away to build new homes for themselves, to shape new lives in foreign land, never to return. Their parents, and in many cases their brothers and sisters, remained behind to face a decade later the Lithuanian Shauleninki and Hitler's hordes.

In Memoriam

We dedicate this page to the memory of those who lost their lives so tragically in the Nazi holocaust.

ת.נ.צ.ב.ה.

The Krakenowo Society in Johannesburg, has, since 1955,
when the date of the massacre was established,
commemorated Yahrzeit for our Martyrs on the Sunday
Night between Rosh Hashana and Yom Kippur
at the Berea Communal Hall.

יזכּור

פרטים וועגן אומקום פון קראַקענאָווער
אידישער קהילה

(איבערגעגעבן טעלעפאָניש דורך מאַטל פאַגור, פון רהאָדעסיע, צו אונדזער
טרעזשורער, זונדל זייוו. יאָהאַנעסבורג).

דעם 22־טן יוני 1941 האָבן דייטשן אָקופירט אונדזער שטאָט
קראַקענאָווע. זיי האָבן גלייך באפוילן די ליטווישע פאַרטיזאַנער
און פּאָליציי צו פאַרזאַמלען אלע יידן אין שול און זיי זאָלן מיט־
נעמען נאָר זאכן וואָס איז נויטיק. איניקע כוליגאַנעס, בפרט איי־
נער מיטן נאָמען דאַמבראָווסקי, האָט גערַאטן אָפּצוזונדערן די
יידישע אָנפירער. זיי האָבן גלייך אָפּגעזונדערט די מוטיקסטע,
צווישן וועלכע עס האָבן זיך געפונען : מאַטל (שלמה־זוסעס)
וואַרקעל, איציק (אפרוימס) לעוויז, פנחס (אפרוימס) לעוויז, אב־
רהם (דעם קאַמאשן־שטעפּערס) פרידמאַן, שמשון שער, שאַבאַן
און נאָך איניקע יונגעלייט און מען האָט זיי אוועקגעשיקט ביים
גלח אויפן באַרג און גלייך דערשאַסן און מיט א בראַנעווע האָבן
זיי פאַרבראַנעוועט דאָס בלוט.

אלע יידן פון קראַקענאָווע האָבן זיי פאַרהאַלטן אין שול איי־
ניקע וואָכן וואו מען האָט זיי גוט אויסגעהונגערט, דאן האָט מען
זיי באפוילן גיין צופוס קיין פּאַנעוועזש און געצוווונגען שלעפּן
פורן און וועגענער, וואו עס האָבן זיך געפונען זייערע קליינע קינ־
דער און זאכן. ווען זיי זיינען געקומען נענטער צו פּאַנעוועזש
האָט מען זיי באפוילן צו פאַרהאַלטן זיך ביים 4־טן פאַלק, צוזא־
מען מיט די אנדערע יידן פון יענע געגנטן. דאָס איז געווען דעם
25־טן טאָג אין חודש אלול (סעפּטעמבער, 1941).

אָט אזוי זיינען אומגעקומען אונדזערע נאָענטסטע און בעס־
טע, וועמענס נעמען וועט קיינמאָל ניט פאַרגעסן ווערן אין אונד־
זערע הערצער.

IN MEMORIAM

Details about the Holocaust of the
Krakenowo Jewish Community.

As related telephonically by Motel Pogur of Rhodesia,
to our Treasurer, Zundel Zive, Johannesburg.

The Germans occupied our town, Krakenowo, on 22 June 1941. They immediately ordered the Lithuanian Partisans and police to gather all the Jews in the shul and instructed them to take only bare necessities with them. Some of the hooligans, especially one named Dambrovsky, suggested separating the Jewish Leaders. They immediately separated the most courageous, among whom were to be found: Mottel (Sh'lomo Zuse's) Varkel, Itzik (Afroim's) Levin, Pinchas (Afroim's) Levin, and Avrom (the bootmaker's) Friedman, Shim'on Sher, Shaban and another few youths, and they sent them away to the Catholic Priest, at the top of the hill, and immediately shot them all and raked over their blood with a harrow.

They detained all the Jews in the school for a few weeks, where they starved them thoroughly and then ordered them to walk to Poneveszh on foot and forced them to haul carts and wagons in which were their little children and belongings.

When they approached Poneveszh, they ordered them to be detained at the 4th regiment, together with the other Jews from that region. This was the 25th of Elul (September 1941).

And so perished our nearest and dearest whose names will never be forgotten and whose memory will never leave our hearts.

A translation of the previous page from Yiddish by Bella Golubchik

A DAY IN KRAKENOWO AFTER THE SECOND WORLD WAR

The writer of this report is Mrs Ida Pogur, who was born in Krakenowo. Together with her husband she lived through the Nazi Purgatory, and managed to survive. They now live in Bulawayo, Rhodesia, together with their family.

We lived through five difficult War years in the Kovno Ghetto, in suffering and pain, hunger and terror, struggling to stay alive, every day, every hour, every minute.

My husband and I, hid in an excavation under the floor, for the last hundred days of the War, with only a sliver of light. In addition to which we were forced to remain sitting all the time, as the hiding place was so small.

One happy day, the sun began to shine again for us. Our brave "peasant woman", who endangered her own life to save us, came to our hiding place; she stretched her hand out to us in kindness and love, and with tears in her eyes, she released us. "You are free ! You are free!" she shouted.

We were drawn back by a great longing to our shtetaleh, Krakenowo, which was so dear to us, and where we had spent the years of our youth. Our boy friends and girl friends had all perished: Chanah Yaivush, Chaya Zelikowitz, Avrom Zelikowitz, Tziviah Levit, Hirsh Rabinowitz, Chatzkeh Chait, Hirshkeh Levin (my brother), Feigeh Pogur (my husband's sister), Yisroel Binder, Shilkeh Levin (my sister), and all the rest of the shtetl, perished.

We used to stroll, singing, dancing freely, in the fields and woods, until late at night; we sang all the Yiddish songs and all the Hebrew songs that we knew, and could never have imagined, that on the morrow, our Christian neighbour would become our Executioner.

One day, Shmulkeh, our young Krakenower Hero, arrived. He had managed to survive the War, with luck and bravery, struggling for his life on the Russian Front. He remained abandoned and alone on earth. While lying on the Front, he promised himself, that if he ever could return to Krakenowo, he would seek vengeance.

He sought out many little Jewish children, who had been hidden with Christian families and brought them back into the Jewish community. Shmulkeh also collected money and erected a large Memorial stone in Poneveszh, in memory of all the Krakenower Jews who had perished in the Poneveszher Ghetto. He achieved a great deal until one day, the Lithuanian Partisans murdered him.

I went back to see our shtetl, Krakenowo, with this great young hero.

It was on a Sunday. The whole market square which had been surrounded by tidy houses was overgrown with wild grasses. Geese foraged and cows grazed there. The shutters of the houses were half shut. It all gave the impression that the peasants were afraid to look the light straight in the eye.

The clear running waters of the Nevyaszeh River, where the Krakenower youth spent its beautiful summer days, had dried up and become overgrown with weeds.

As I have already mentioned, we arrived on a Sunday and the church bells began to toll. With trembling legs and bile in my throat, with tears and pain and bowed head, I suddenly became empowered. I suppressed the tears, raised my head high, and with my remaining strength walked to the church and waited for the congregation to come out, to show them that they could not annihilate the Jewish People.

When they saw us, many of the Christians retreated in fright. Many of them fell at my feet and made the sign of the Cross and wept. They couldn't believe that a few of the Krakenower Jews still remained alive.

I was overcome by fear and trembling, I could barely walk back to the automobile and with eyes shut tight, begged Shmulkeh to hurry and leave our shtetl, Krakenowo, for which we yearned with nostalgia and where we had spent the days of our youth.

Translated by Bella Golubchik

A photograph of the Zive family and friends taken in 1934, in Krakenowo.
Top row: Right to left: Ben Zion Zive, Pessah Chayah Gil, Itzik Gil, Faivel's wife and daughter, P'ninah Zive (now Mrs Kaplan- Johannesburg), A student from the Slabodka Yeshivah, Tanya Kruger (now Katzan – Johannesburg), wife of Lewis Katzen (deceased in Johannesburg).
Bottom row: Bezalel Resnick, Rodel Resnick (Johannesburg) wife of Moshe Gershon Resnick (died in Lithuania), Rabbi Wolf Kuznetz and Rivel Kuznetz (died in Lithuania), Wolf and Chayah Soreh Zive (died in Johannesburg) and Chayah Zelda Kruger (Johannesburg).

א מערקווירדיקער חלום

א מערקווירדיקער חלום האָט זיך געחלומט אונדזער
לאַנדסמאַן זונדל זיוו, דאָ אין אפריקע. דעם 30־טן יוני
1941 האָט ער געזען אין חלום זיין שוועסטער חיה רייוועל
קוזנעץ, צחאַמען מיט איר מאַן הרב וואָלף קוזנעץ, זייער
טעכטערל בײלע און זונעלע הירשעלע, אלע לויפֿנדיק.
פלוצלונג האָט ער געזען ווי זיין שוועסטער פֿאַרלירט אײן
האַנט, און אין באלד זיינען זיי אלע פֿאַרשוואונדן. אין א צווייטן
חלום, דעם 25־טן אויגוסט, האָט זיך די שוועסטער ווידער
באוויזן, און א דריטן מאָל דעם 8־טן פעברואר 1942.

A REMARKABLE DREAM

Our landsman, Zundel Zive, dreamed a remarkable dream, here in South Africa.

On 30 June 1941, he dreamed that his sister, Chaya Reizel Kuznetz, her husband Rabbi Wolf Kuznetz, their little daughter Beilah and son Hirshaleh, were all running away.

Suddenly, he saw his sister, losing one of her hands – and then they all immediately disappeared.

In a second dream, on 25 August 1941, his sister reappeared. She then appeared to him in a dream on 8 February 1942 for a third time.

Translated by Bella Golubchik

HISTORY OF THE KRAKENOWO SICK BENEFIT AND BENEVOLENT SOCIETY

A total of £35,000 has been lent out to members since the Krakenowo Society was founded 60 years ago – and there is still money in the kitty for deserving causes.

Today of course, proper ledgers and other books of accounts are used by the secretary and treasurer in their financial dealings; but way back in the nostalgic early days David Rottanberg, first Treasurer of the Society, had an easier and perhaps just as effective way of doing things.

In charge of the Sick Fund, he committed to memory the figures of income and expenditure. In complicated transactions, he wrote the figures down on the starched cuffs of his shirt. When queried in the street about an item of expenditure, Reb David would roll up his jacket sleeve and read the figures from the shirt cuff.

Reb David was one of the founders of the Krakenowo Society when it was officially established in Johannesburg in 1901, but the origins really began in Cape Town two years earlier. It was at the home of Mr. Ely Joselovitz (father in law of the present chairman, Mr J Goldman) that the decision was taken to form a Society known as the Aushei Achei Ezer D' Krakenowo.

Little is known about the activities of the landsleit in the period following that informal first meeting in Cape Town, except that that was where the embryo was first conceived.

When there began a drift of landsleit up to Johannesburg, led by Mr. Mane Jochelson and Mr Isser Cohen, scope existed for the formation of a Society on the Rand ... and it is the 60th anniversary of the founding of the Society in the home of Mr Boruch Smith that is being commemorated this evening.

Mr. Jochelson was elected the first chairman, and the founding committee included Messrs Isser Cohen, Louis Seeff, Isaac Salamon, Boruch Smith, David Rottanberg, Isaac Green, Ely Joselovitz, A Bessarabia and Zelik Isaac Levin.

Newly arrived immigrants who founded the Krakenowo Society in Johannesburg in 1901

(And what a tribute it is to the fervour of those early pioneers that in many cases their children are today the active workers on the Krakenowo Committee, less busy perhaps than in those early formative years when immigration from Lithuania swelled to a steady, unabating stream, but no less dedicated).

The main activity was to help sick landsleit and also those newly arrived immigrants who were short of funds, know how and friends.

In almost all cases these immigrants from far off Krakenowo were unmarried men, consequently lacking home attention should they fall ill. The Society set up a Sick Fund which offered free medical treatment, medicine, hospitalisation if necessary-and daily attendance by two members of the committee.

Two of the most indefatigable of these workers were the late Isser Cohen and the late Zelik Isaac Levin. Cheerful, always ready to help, these two would sit for hours at the bedside of a sick landsman, be it daytime or nigh time, bringing him solace and much needed company.

Scores of acts like this gave true meaning to the word "chavershaft", and the Rand Jewish community is richer for the efforts of Isser Cohen and Zelik Isaac Levin and their colleagues.

It was in this early era of altruism that the above mentioned tale of Reb David Rottanberg's shirt cuff transactions played its part. As new landsmen stepped off the ships in Cape Town and entrained for Johannesburg and the Reef, so did the demands for help multiply.

Not quite as big, perhaps, as some other landmanshaften, the Krakenowo Society was one of the pioneers of them all, and one of the most dedicated in its work.

In 1910 the Society founded a Gemilus Chesed for loans. Mr S Flaum was the Organiser and first chairman of that committee. As no funds were readily available, a hundred shares of £1 each were issued and a "capital" of £ 100 was raised. The first loan to be granted was for the sum of £7.10.0 against two securities.

To swell the Society's coffers, dances and other functions were held at the old Wanderers Hall near the Johannesburg Station, and income from High Festival Services also went to the Gemilus Chesed.

Address by the Chairman, Mr Jack Goldman, at the Golden Jubilee

These Services began after a move in 1908 to import a Sefer Torah from Krakenowo. Baal Tefilah of the first minyans was Mr. Hirshe Hershowitz, father of the late mining magnate, .S Hersov.

During World War One Krakenowo landsleit established their own war fund in aid of Jews who had been banished to Russia, and later for the assistance of Jews who returned to their almost ruined town of Krakenowo in Lithuania.

After the end of hostilities in 1918, the influx of immigrants to the Union was resumed, and money went to the needy and the sick.

Presentation made at the Golden Jubilee to the late Mr and Mrs L Seeff, distinguished Foundation members of the Krakenowo Society, by Mt Barney Levin (Secretary).

In 1934, M. Jacob Goldman was elected chairman of the Society. Although born in Lithuania, he was what one might term a "second generation" member, taking up office when the ranks of his elders

Executive of the Society at the time of the Golden Jubilee

*Standing: Dr Harvey Cohen, late Willie Cohen, late Louis Kotzen, Jack Perilly, Morris Bass and Barney Lax.
Sitting: Nathan Esra, Ike Broide, Jack Goldman (Chairman), Woolf Cohen, Sydney Seeff and Barney Levin.*

Combined Ladies' and Men's Committee of the Golden Jubilee.

gradually began to thin. (In this he was typical of others e.g. gradually Wolfie Cohen, son of Isser Cohen, as vice chairman, took an active part to follow the fine example of his father; Ike Broude, son in law of Isser Cohen, was honorary treasurer for many years; and so did Barney Levin, son of Zelik Isaac Levin, who has been honorary secretary for 35 years; and also Mrs J Perilly and Mrs B Lax, children of the Society's first chairman. Mr M Jochelson; also Mrs A Gulgut, daughter of Mr S Levin; Natie Esra, son in law of Mr B Smith, as honorary secretary for 26 years.)

A nephew, who is also the son in law of Mr and Mrs E Joselovitz, Mr Goldman became a dedicated worker in their tradition and he remains chairman after 27 years unbroken service in this role. In all he has been a member for 52 years.

Ray Smith has been one of the joint honorary secretaries for about 10 years.

During World War II, a war fund similar to that organised 25 years before was inaugurated, in the hope that the Krakenowo community could be helped after the end of hostilities. But, alas, Krakenowo Jewry was destroyed by the Nazis.

Only very occasionally did news filter through from Europe of the survival of a lonely Krakenowo man or woman or child, but whenever and wherever possible the Society's war fund played its part. We were one of the first institutions to be affiliated to the S A Jewish Board of Deputies.

Such was the desire of its members to help others. That on occasion, donations have been made to the Israel United Appeal and also to the Magen David Adom and we are also members for 30 years of the Kosher Kitchen and Jewish Orphanage.

As for the Torah specially imported from Krakenowo, this is still in use, at the Sydenham Highlands North Hebrew Congregation.

In 1945 we celebrated our 45th anniversary with a social and dance at the H.O.D. Hall.

Tens years ago, when the Krakenowo Society held its Golden Jubilee in Johannesburg, it was announced that since its inception, the Society had lent out a total of £30,000 to needy cases. That total has now risen to £35,000 – a sure sign that, despite the passage of time, the Krakenowo Society still fulfils an important role in the local Jewish Community.

The most active member of our Society at present in Sydney Seeff our honorary Treasurer and his wife Naomi, at whose home our meetings have been held for the past 12 years.

Executive Committee at the time of the Diamond Jubilee

Back: Nathan Esrachowitz, Ray Smith and Barney Levin (Secretaries).
Front: Sydney Seeff (Treasurer), Jack Goldman (Chairman) and Woolf Cohen (Vice Chairman).

KRAKENOWO SOCIETY DIAMOND JUBILEE

Seeff and Morris Seeff.

Committee

Front row: Cherry Gell, Stanley Seeff and Laz Tocher.

Second row: Nathan Esrachowitz, Hilda Lax, Sydney Seeff, Jack Goldman (Chairman), Woolf Cohen, Ray Smith and Berney Levin.

Third row: Barney Lax, Minnie Gell, Florence Perilly, Naomi Seeff, Fanny Goldman and Annie Galgut.

Back row: Isaac Gell, Jack Perilly, Pearl Tocher, Ted Tocher, Blume Levin, Dora

Ladies' Committee

Front: Ray Smith, Florence Perilly, Fanny Goldman, Cherry Gell, Annie Galgut and Dora Seeff.

Back: Naomi Seeff, Hilda Lax, Pearl Tocher, Minnie Gell, Blume Levin and Esther Tocher

FALKOW BROS (Pty) Ltd
Footwear Distributors

NU-TILITIES
Supplier of cleaning requirements

RAPID TIMBER SUPPLIES
Stockists of South African Pine

E EW HOCHFELD
New and second hand bags and pockets and twine and rope

PERCY AND BELLA ZELIKOW

MILLERS ELECTRICAL LINES (Pty) Limited

PEARCE AND ALLEN (Pty) Ltd
Panda Industrial Gloves and Protective Clothing

S A MINING SUPPLIES PTY LTD
Verbus high-tensile bolts

S G NORMAN & CO (Pty) Ltd
Registered Certified Sanitary Engineers

HIGH COURT PROVISIONS
Mr and Mrs I Sacks

SYDMORE EMGINEERING WORKS (Pty) Limited
Manufacturing Engineers

CARDBOARD PACKING UTILITIES (Pty) Limited
Corrugated Containers

S P Q R STOES - Mr and Mrs E Ries and Family

ATLAS SCREW CO (Pty) Limited
Fasteners for all industries

C F INDUSTRIES (Pty) Limited
Sheet metal Products

RANCE, COLLY & CO (Pty) Limited
Mining, Engineering and Industrial Supplies

BARRIS BROS (Pty) Limited

JEPPE SUBWAY PHARMACY - K Hurwitz MPS
The grandson of Avrom Lazar